Enjoy Flynnie's Tournament!

[signature] 2007

MISFITS ON THE LINKS

MISFITS ON THE LINKS

A GOLFER'S GUIDE TO FREAKS ALONG THE FAIRWAY

JOEL ZUCKERMAN

ILLUSTRATED BY JEFF WONG

Andrews McMeel Publishing, LLC

Kansas City

06 07 08 09 10 SDB 10 9 8 7 6 5 4 3 2

ISBN-13: 978-0-7407-5706-8

ISBN-10: 0-7407-5706-7

Library of Congress Control Number: 2005933799

Book design by Kelly & Company, Lee's Summit, Missouri

www.andrewsmcmeel.com

ATTENTION: SCHOOLS AND BUSINESSES
Andrews McMeel books are available at quantity discounts with bulk purchase for educational, business, or sales promotional use. For information, please write to: Special Sales Department, Andrews McMeel Publishing, LLC, 4520 Main Street, Kansas City, Missouri 64111.

To a thousand different hackers,
whackers, slackers, yakkers, and crackers
that inspired my imagination.

And to Paul deVere of Hilton Head Island,
who inspired the book.

Contents

Acknowledgments

Years ago I submitted an irreverent essay on non-playing wives (the essence of which is found within these pages) to a magazine I was contributing to with some regularity. I began this diatribe by listing some of the contemptible characters I'd encountered over time, then went on to say there was no one as remotely annoying as a non-playing wife. My editor at the time wasn't much interested in my overall thesis but was intrigued by the listing of miscreants I ticked off at the beginning—the club throwers, turf gougers, shadow casters, cart gunners, mismarkers, etc.

Focusing on this unexpected tangent, he commissioned a tongue-in-cheek field guide and hired the estimable Jeff Wong to illustrate my imaginary (but far too real) characters. The magazine folded shortly thereafter, and we've had little contact in the interim. But my sincere thanks to Cameron Morfit, who was the original inspiration for the characters that come to life in the following pages.

Also a nod of recognition to my neighborhood "Hardi Boys," twins Trevor and Drew Hardigan, who improved my sophomoric Pig Latin immeasurably, and helped with the Latin translations of these various misfits.

My only brother is my favorite agent. Or my only agent is my favorite brother—it doesn't really matter how you say it. But thanks to Al Zuckerman of Writers House, who finally found a literary project of mine salable. Let's hope he's right.

Despite my vagabond nature, I stay true to my roots and play plenty of golf with my permanent (albeit distant) posse—Moonie the Gagaroonie, "Nine Fingers" Nadelman, Sandy Andy, Easy Eduardo, and Ms. Glare-All and her long-suffering spouse, Captain Rivi. You may be misfits, but you're *my* misfits.

To my girls—Elaine, Karli, and Kayla, who'll never be misfits on the links, mainly because they stay within the confines of the tennis court.

And lastly, to Kyle Poplin, who took a flier on my writing ability almost a decade ago. What would I be doing today without that long-ago vote of confidence? Not writing golf books, that's practically a certainty.

Introduction

Just like you, I love to play golf. Perhaps unlike you, I've played and continue to play regularly with an incredibly wide range of golfers of different ages, backgrounds, abilities, geographies, attitudes, incomes, philosophies, and habits. Sure, I have my regular cronies, normal foursomes, and favorite golf buddies. But as a travel writer and avowed vagabond golfer, I'm often thrust into brand-new situations with folks who introduce themselves on the first tee.

Most of these experiences are rewarding. Others are less so. But the sheer number of people I've encountered over the years made me realize there are definite "types" out there trolling the fairways, often the rough, and occasionally the woods of our sixteen thousand some-odd courses.

So with the help of illustrator nonpareil Jeff Wong, I offer you a golfer's guide to your local links. It doesn't matter if your home track is like Augusta, Disgusta, or somewhere in the vast middle, because the types of folks you're about to meet are universal. This handy guide fits easily into your golf bag and will help you identify in moments all of the regular denizens of virtually any course in the nation.

A brief word of warning: While almost every species described herein is inherently friendly and relatively domesticated, always use common sense. If they are aggravated, intimidated, or otherwise riled, there's always the chance of a violent reaction. Remember to keep your distance, at least initially, and always be respectful of any new species you encounter.

MISFITS ON THE LINKS

THE BALL HAWK

Carpe strata 👉 Nobody likes to waste bullets. Whether you spend $5 or $50 a dozen, any player lacking a full-time bag toter or without their name stitched into their golf bag is reluctant to let a pellet go, at least not without a cursory search. The key word is *cursory*. Ball Hawks have a strain of obsessive-compulsive disorder. They may not wash their hands every ten minutes or repeatedly check to see if the house is locked before work, but in a way their affliction is worse. They hold up the golf course ad infinitum, searching desperately for a bargain-bin castoff that no amount of cleaning will ever restore past the color of dull parchment. If it's in the lagoon they're ready to put on waders. If it's in the woods they'll don mosquito netting. These wackos need a cold dose of reality, the type once administered to me by my good pal Rhino. Whining a bit after taking some time looking for a shiny Top-Flite, I explained that normally I wouldn't waste time on the task, but the ball was brand new. "No it isn't," rebuked the twice-a-year golfer, harshly. "You already hit it once." True enough, upon reflection.

BEHAVIOR Spends as much time weed whacking and lagoon sifting as he does swinging.

MARKINGS Pockets bulging with so many found balls he looks like a victim of a tropical disease. Carries two styles of ball retrievers.

CALL "I swear it was coming in right on this line."

CARPE STRATA

THE BEVERAGE CART KEWPIE

Amstel damsel ☞ For some golfers, getting tanked from tee to green is half the fun. The Beverage Cart Kewpie is integral to these proceedings. These college-age gals circle the course in their snack and drink buggies, waving ubiquitously, craving eye contact with an army of mostly bedraggled and indifferent golfers. But every so often they hit the mother lode. It might be four guys, sometimes eight. If the stars align, even twelve or sixteen, playing in a group outing. They swarm and surround her like tykes encircling a department-store Santa. Is the potential tip windfall worth the ogling, ridiculous come-ons, trite pickup lines, shameless double entendres, lame jokes, and, after the inevitable rebuffing, the insults or disparaging comments? Only the Kewpie knows for sure.

BEHAVIOR Like a sexy Good Humor man, she circles the "neighborhood" endlessly. She doles out adult beverages and snappy comebacks, dispenses sugary treats and endures sugary smooth talk, sells salty snacks and ignores salty language.

MARKINGS Halter tops, hair bands, wide smile, short shorts.

CALL "I'd love to sell you the entire cooler of Bud Light, but I can only sell three beers per person at a time. Sure we take credit cards. Would you like to leave an imprint? Sorry, I have a boyfriend."

AMSTEL DAMSEL

BIGFOOT

Terra rupturas ☞ This category has little to do with actual size or girth. For example, my teenage daughter and some of her friends are lovely and petite creatures, seeking out their haute couture in the "Small" section at their favorite fashion haunts. But when they descend the wooden staircase in clogs they sound like a herd of elephants or a massive avalanche. Actually it's a combination—an avalanche of elephants. On the golf course, we can be thankful this disturbing phenomenon is still a rarity. You might be paired with a fellow who can't quite get his feet off the ground while walking around the green, and the rake marks he leaves with his soft spikes are literally and figuratively a drag. Even more uncommon (and undesirable) is the gent who somehow exerts more pounds per square inch of pressure upon the delicate turf than it appears he's able to. The result is a green with the type of distinct footprints one rarely encounters outside of an Arthur Murray Dance Studio.

MARKINGS Bozo shoes with penny nails for golf spikes.

BEHAVIOR Steadies himself over a ten-foot putt by anchoring into the turf like he's trying to win the long drive contest.

CALL "Some people are always bitching about spike marks and bumpy greens, but not me. I just put a solid stroke on it, and wherever it ends up it ends up."

TERRA RUPTURAS

THE BOOZEHOUND

Brewski gulpus ☛ Playing golf and drinking beer are among my favorite hobbies, though they're rarely indulged concurrently. The rationale is twofold. First, it takes every ounce of energy and concentration for me to navigate the links efficiently. Despite this self-imposed sobriety, too often the final scorecard tally is a number closer to body temperature than par. Second, I'm a believer in the 19th hole. Here in the cool conviviality of the tavern, or on the back deck overlooking the final green, one indulges in a couple of icy beers while recounting the triumphs and traumas of the completed round. But not everyone feels the same way. Mellow fellows lubricate with a beer or two per round. Those who rely on "swing oil" to keep their game together indulge in a couple per side. But the real problem child is that boozing nuisance who indulges in a beer or two per hole.

MARKINGS Depending on the temperature, carries a portable cooler, flask, or wineskin.

CALL "God, it's hot out here. Where's the quench wench? She hasn't been around for at least three holes!"

BEHAVIOR Gives credit card imprint to the Beverage Cart Kewpie (page 4); blames poor play on killer hangover.

BREWSKI GULPUS

THE CAFFEINE FIEND

Java glutto ☛ Golf should be a game of unhurried tranquillity. Avid players enjoy the familiar camaraderie of the group, the easygoing banter, and the chance to relax amid nature's beauty. And then there's the Fiend. Whether his vice is caffeine or nicotine, his goal is to make it from first tee to final green as quickly as possible. He races around the course and paces the tee box like an expectant father outside the delivery room. He twitches over putts and bitches if there's a minimal delay caused by the group ahead. Being called a "grinder" on the golf course is a compliment; it refers to those who can bear down and score well without their best swing. But the only grinder that concerns pathetic Marlboro Man is the one that turns coffee beans into particles. He's got an excuse for making a double bogey on the 9th. He was looking ahead to the double espresso he'd be ordering at the turn.

BEHAVIOR Eschews practice swings, walks ahead of other players, fiddles with his lighter, deposits cigarette butts in bunkers.

MARKINGS Carries a Styrofoam cup, thermos, or cigarette carton.

CALL "This pace of play is killing me. We've been out here for almost two hours and we're just starting the back nine!"

JAVA GLUTTO

THE CAREER CADDIE

Afinis artificium ☞ He's not a part-timer, but a lifer. He's not a teenager bagging it on weekends for beer and gas money, or a college kid on semester break. The only learning institution he's attended is the school of hard knocks. He's not an aspiring mini-tour pro, or an up-and-coming business executive moonlighting for a few extra bucks until his career kicks into overdrive. You can find them in the States, but here they're as rare as links courses. Pine Valley and Winged Foot are caddie bastions back east, Pebble Beach, Cypress Point, and Bandon Dunes out west. But to find the real deal? You must head to the U.K. They often smell like they bathed in a barrel of Bushmills, have a mouthful of broken china, and are as worn and leathery as a 1950s catcher's mitt. The brogue is thick and the trousers are worn thin, but they know the game almost as well as they know the course on which they guide you. And because their razor wit gets far more use than the razor for their chin, they can add immeasurably to the enjoyment and experience of the round.

BEHAVIOR They list to the side as they walk the fairways; decades of shouldering a forty-pound staff bag causes them to veer like the proverbial shopping cart with one bad wheel.

MARKINGS In the U.S. they often wear white jump-suits that, were they orange, would be identical to prison garb. Overseas they dress more like classics professors who've spent a week living outdoors above a steam grate.

CALL "Aye, sir, that's quite the bag of high-tech equipment you have there. Tell me, is this your first time at a Scottish golf course, or just a golf course in general?"

AFINIS ARTIFICIUM

THE CART GUNNER

Supersonicus mario ☞ While his more skillful colleagues might've been on the high school golf team, he was taking metal shop. The guys he plays with as an adult spent youthful summers in the caddie yard, but he worked at the local garage. Before he came to the game he was more familiar with a dipstick than a driver, a T-Bird than a tee shot. He thought the words "clutch" and "choke" were nouns referring to the mechanism that connects an engine to a transmission system, and an air-flow valve, respectively. It wasn't until he started spending time out of the grease pit and on the greensward that he realized they refer to those who can and cannot handle the pressure of a down-to-the-wire Nassau.

MARKINGS Youthful models often drive muscle cars like Corvettes and Camaros. Older versions (Latin name: *Midlife criseum*) have either Porsches or Jaguar convertibles.

BEHAVIOR Either slams brakes or guns gas pedal at the top of your backswing; often causes whiplash by accelerating before passenger is fully seated.

CALL "This cart is so damn pokey! I wish I could take off the governor."

SUPERSONICUS MARIO

THE CAVEMAN

Brutus forcus ☞ Picture NBA superstar Yao Ming alongside "Mini Me" actor Verne Troyer. The former is a seven-foot Asian with a full shock of hair, the latter a three-foot American with a shiny pate. But these two are practically twins compared to the Caveman and his polar opposite, Mr. "Piddle-Down-the-Middle" (page 60). The Caveman has one simple objective: hitting every golf shot with maximum force. To borrow a military phrase of recent vintage, his preferred game is "Shock and Awe" golf. To wit: He wants to awe you with his length, but it's a shock when the ball actually remains in play for more than two or three shots consecutively. Everything about this fellow is oversized: his physical presence, his driver, his ego, his capacity for risk. There's not a par-5 on the course he won't go for in two. There's not a tree he doesn't think he can launch one over. He's less concerned with score than "soar." He wants to hit it big—he'll tell you so, bust a gut in the attempt, and every so often catapult his tee ball right down the fairway to that mythical 300-yard mark. But mostly his unabashed efforts lead to screaming pull hooks that bounce out of bounds or towering pop-ups that threaten to bring rain. He's fun enough to play with, particularly as an opponent.

MARKINGS Extralong driver, extralong tees.

BEHAVIOR Swings so hard it causes a wind tunnel effect on the tee box. Takes divots so deep they could break an ankle.

CALL "You hit a seven-iron into the green? Watch me get there with a wedge."

BRUTUS FORCUS

THE "CELL" MATE

Moto rola ☞ Ah, technology. If we're not wired, we're potentially fired, so harried execs arm themselves with every gadget that comes down the pike. Once the golf course was a place to relax and retreat from workday pressures, but no longer. Instant access and availability are the watchwords, and a cell phone is as essential as a fresh sleeve of balls for far too many golfers who've supposedly stolen away to the links for an afternoon "off." But fortunately there are indications of revolution. NO CELL PHONES ALLOWED is a sign that's popping up at finer facilities more often. It began in the grill room, where animated one-way conversations were drowning out the essential banter of birdies, bets, and bogeys. This mentality has spread to other areas of the club, and there are signs it might someday make it to the greensward itself. And if that day ever occurs, our supposed progress will regress to the game's most enduring positive qualities: peace and quiet.

BEHAVIOR Rushes back to the cart to retrieve messages, records memos between shots, occasionally putts one-handed with phone tucked under chin.

MARKINGS High-tech equipment, including a digital pager, Palm Pilot, and tri-mode, fold-up phone. Golf clubs are pretty decent as well.

CALL "I can't stand it myself when guys bring phones on the course, but I'm trying to close a major deal here."

MOTO ROLA

THE CHATTERBOX

Incessa locqua ☞ One might equate this human toothache to the Storyteller (page 76). While she is a second cousin twice removed to that blatherer, her true blood relation is actually the Snackman (page 70). Think about it. In both cases the mouth is constantly moving, though nothing good ever comes of it. At least the junk goes *in* the Snackman's maw, which doesn't really hurt anyone but him. This is in contrast to the incessant inanity dribbling from the lips of this poor wretch. Who's to say why she can't shut up for ten consecutive seconds, infringing upon, some might go so far as to say ruining, the quietude that is one of the attractions of the game to begin with? Uncomfortable in her own skin? Blissfully unaware of the protocol of the game? Born without the benefit of the essential filter between brain and mouth that most humans possess? Maybe it's all three. Too bad she can't spend her leisure hours on the psychiatrist's couch finding out, instead of riding shotgun in the cart, offering opinions, spouting clichés, and buzzing in your ear like a mosquito. In her favor, at least she's not a blood-sucking parasite. On the other hand, you can swat a mosquito and nobody cares.

MARKINGS Comes in all shapes and sizes, but tendencies are to the extremes — usually either an ectomorph or endomorph. Lips are often chapped from profuse flapping.

CALL "Never up never in my what a beautiful day I gotta get to the restroom aren't these new golf shoes precious but they hurt my feet oh look at that robin want a sip of my soda I think George Clooney is the most . . ."

BEHAVIOR Emits a constant stream of babble during the course of a round. She talks before, during, and after almost every shot of her own, and darn near everyone else's.

INCESSA LOCQUA

THE COCKEYED OPTIMIST

Erro consolatio ☞ Golfers come in all sorts of annoying varieties, but among the most insidious characters is the chronic Cockeyed Optimist. The moment you crack your tee shot you hear one of these nut jobs start crowing, "Center cut! That one is straight as a string." Every approach shot is greeted with a triumphant cry of, "That's gonna hit the flagstick!" A forty-foot putt might be halfway to the hole and this bag of gas is wildly gesticulating, while nonsensically yelling "Drano!" Little does it matter that the aforementioned drive veered into the woods, the supposed deadly approach drifted into a bunker, and the putt wobbled to a feeble conclusion a full eight feet short. Apparently, this guy never got enough love at home. And in his efforts to win friends and please his playing partners he natters on incessantly about the wonderful caliber of our mostly mediocre golf shots. Fortunately, there's a simple one word solution that will help you deal with this maniac: earplugs.

MARKINGS Pasted-on smile, rose-colored glasses.

BEHAVIOR An abundance of backslapping, quickly followed by backpedaling.

CALL "Wow. I could've sworn you were going to knock it stiff. I can't believe that ball plopped short of the green into the water. Do you think there's some wind up there?"

ERRO CONSOLATIO

THE CLUB CHUCKER

Ira javelina ☛ A round of golf is an emotional roller-coaster, and different personality traits often emerge. Some golfers are tranquil, others gregarious, some lively, and others withdrawn. And some are downright angry. The anger manifests itself in different ways. Swearing is the standard, more common than foot stomping or turf kicking. Most ill-tempered golfers aren't inherently dangerous, save for the Club Chucker. There's probably not a player alive that hasn't whipped an offending instrument down the fairway. In any 19th hole players tell tales of crazies, who in a fit of pique tossed clubs into tree branches, the underbrush, or a nearby water hazard. Fortunately, most such players mature and amend their ways. They learn to leave their cutoff jeans at home, the colored golf balls in the bargain bin, and their clubs in the bag. But some never learn.

BEHAVIOR Usually profane. The wild species releases clubs in helicopter fashion, endangering those around him, while the domestic species often just submerges the club into the turf.

MARKINGS Shirt often untucked; chronic cases exhibit massive muscle buildup in shoulder girdle.

CALL "Watch it! Sorry about that, but try and stay to my side after a bad shot."

IRA JAVELINA

THE COLLECTOR

Aparatus coactor ☞ Some kids liked baseball; he liked the cards. Other kids chased butterflies; he pinned them on cork board. The neighborhood delinquents tossed rocks; he gathered and sorted them by type. As an adult, his passion and his weekend pastime have fused into a dangerous combination. His Achilles' heel might be logo tees or logo balls. Perhaps it's scorecards, ball markers, divot-repair tools, caps, money clips, umbrellas, golf towels, or shirts. The particular addiction doesn't matter, because the motivation is always the same. For most golfers, the day's incomplete until walking off the final green. But for this harmless, often charmless fellow, it's "game over" walking to the first tee, provided he's enjoyed a successful hunt in the pro shop beforehand.

BEHAVIOR Examines the pencils on all rental carts; always borrowing divot-repair tools to check for unusual logos.

MARKINGS Normally uses a lightweight stand-bag, but always arrives with an additional duffle bag or rolling suitcase.

CALL "Is that ball mark from Ballybunion? I'll trade you an Old Course scorecard and a Carnoustie towel still in the wrapper!"

APARATUS COACTOR

THE CRETIN

Tifdwarf rex ☞ Does it irk you to see someone toss a cigarette butt out a car window? A Cretin is likely to dump the entire ashtray into the middle of the road. Golfers like this just don't care. Period. How can one even count the ways they offend on the links? They might be clattering around at the ball washer, blithely cleansing their orb (often a stolen striper in the most insidious cases) at the exact moment you begin your backswing. They are of the mindset that the shortest distance between their ball and the cup is directly across your putting line, and not one in a hundred would be considered light on their feet. They don't pick up a flagstick, they don't pick up a bar tab, they don't pick up the cart girl, but unlike the first two examples, the last is not for lack of trying. Ability is irrelevant, but think of the classiest golfer you know of, maybe a Bobby Jones, Byron Nelson, or Jack Nicklaus. Now think of the polar opposite. That's your classic Cretin.

MARKINGS Metal spikes, extralong ball retriever, tube socks.

BEHAVIOR Takes beaver-pelt divots, trudges through bunkers, and drags feet on the greens.

CALL "I don't really make ball marks."

TIFDWARF REX

THE CRYBABY

Whinus continuous ☞ Life has dealt this complainer a bad hand. Or so he tells his playing partners. He might as well have the words "Why Me?" tattooed across his forehead, so quickly does he find fault with a passing cloud, an unexpected breeze, the sudden birdsong coming from a nearby tree. He goes through life wearing puce-colored glasses. He loves Da Vinci's enigmatic painting, the Moaner Lisa. His all-time favorite movie is *The Days of Whiner Roses*. His name might not be Murphy, but he's a staunch proponent of Murphy's Law nonetheless.

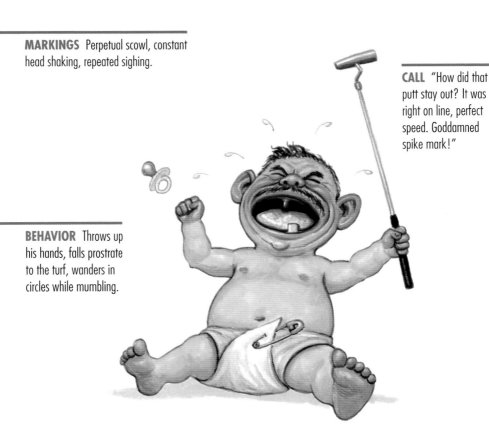

MARKINGS Perpetual scowl, constant head shaking, repeated sighing.

CALL "How did that putt stay out? It was right on line, perfect speed. Goddamned spike mark!"

BEHAVIOR Throws up his hands, falls prostrate to the turf, wanders in circles while mumbling.

WHINUS CONTINUOUS

THE FAIR-WEATHER FAIRY

Homo tempestas sollicitudo ☞ Remember the lame one-liner popularized by the late Bob Hope? He used to say, "I play golf in the mid-seventies. Any warmer than that and I won't go out." This is the essence of the Fair-Weather Fairy. He claims to love the game, but the atmospheric conditions have to be just right for him to actually participate. If it's too warm or cold, too soggy or arid, too cloudy, gusty, humid, hazy, foggy, muddy, or dusty, he'll pass. If the greens have been top-dressed, aerated, verticut, or punched, forget it. If the fairways are dormant, overseeded, or sketchy, don't bother calling. If it's Super Bowl Sunday, Masters weekend, U.S. Open week, or Breakfast at Wimbledon, he'll pass. He's a distasteful combination of diffident and difficult, which is really too bad. Because the three or four times a year when the weather is perfect and he'll actually come to the golf course, he's a pretty good guy.

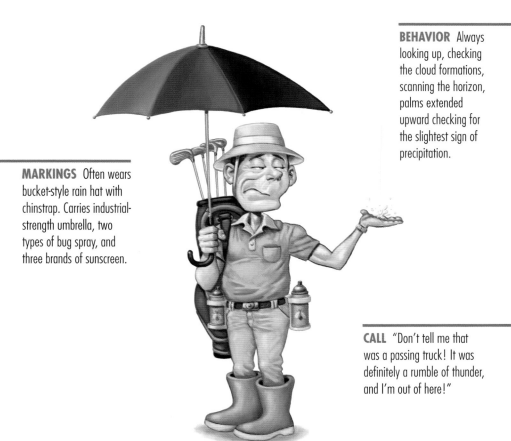

BEHAVIOR Always looking up, checking the cloud formations, scanning the horizon, palms extended upward checking for the slightest sign of precipitation.

MARKINGS Often wears bucket-style rain hat with chinstrap. Carries industrial-strength umbrella, two types of bug spray, and three brands of sunscreen.

CALL "Don't tell me that was a passing truck! It was definitely a rumble of thunder, and I'm out of here!"

HOMO TEMPESTAS SOLLICITUDO

THE FASHION PLATE

Vestis experta 👉 If you can't play good, at least you can look good. This is the philosophy of the Fashion Plate, who venerates Versace, worships at the altar of Armani, and adores the goddess Givenchy. She's not particularly coordinated, but she's certainly color-coordinated. Anyone can match their glove and visor in the same hue, but it takes a peculiar devotion to ensure the color of the grips, shoes, and sweater vest all work together seamlessly. Only the discerning eye notices that her head covers have the same color accents as the panels on her calf-skin golf bag. Her wide-brimmed chapeau cost as much as your high-tech driver. Her angora pullover with silk trim was more expensive than your entire set of graphite-shafted irons. She's tougher to take than a triple bogey, but here's the good news: To avoid looking rumpled, wrinkled, or wilted, she normally packs it in after nine holes.

MARKINGS She dresses like she belongs on a model's runway; twice a season she'll split the fairway.

BEHAVIOR She doesn't smooth the bunker sand because she's busy smoothing her skirt. She doesn't fix divots or ball marks; she fixes her makeup instead.

CALL "This goatskin golf glove is a limited edition Dior! I'm just sorry you can't see my fabulous new manicure."

VESTIS EXPERTA

THE FOOT WEDGER

Genus cheats ☞ This guy vies with the Sandbagger (page 66) for the lowest of the low. The best way of describing the difference is that the 'Bagger is committing grand larceny, while this lowlife is a petty thief. He has as many ways of defrauding his opponent as there are holes on the course. Hell, as there are blades of grass on the tee box. He'll strategically place the cart between his opponent and the ball, the better to surreptitiously improve his lie without detection. He'll switch to his favorite "putting ball" on the green and maybe toss his ball mark toward the hole to get closer to the cup, instead of marking appropriately. Chronic cases affect a ruse where he dislodges sand from the bunker with a phony golf swing, while simultaneously tossing the ball onto the putting surface. Golf requires tremendous concentration. Too bad you also have to concentrate on quelling his antics if you hope for a fair match.

MARKINGS Beady eyes, furtive manner, carries custom golf pencil with eraser.

BEHAVIOR Never loses a ball, miraculously avoids hazards, somehow finds openings through thick trees to advance ball toward green.

CALL "Oh, you're right. That was a 7, not a 6. I forgot about that little chip shot."

GENUS CHEATS

THE GADGET GEEK

Technus obsessus 👉 He's a walking, talking Sharper Image catalog. It's not so much an obsession with the clubs themselves, but the various accoutrements, that really make this Poindexter pant. He's got the latest handheld range finder, calibrated to provide precise distances to the green and every hazard, though he never knows if he'll get the ball airborne or in which direction it might be headed. He has cool X-ray specs that make a ball camouflaged in the underbrush shine like a neon sign. He carries a stretching pole, an umbrella with a built-in seat, a laser putting device, a scientific gizmo that finds the ball's equilibrium, and a lightweight Gore-Tex rain suit that compresses to the size of a deck of cards. He has a miniature digital camera, disposable cornstarch tees, and a combination divot-repair tool/cigar cutter that would set off alarms at airport security counters worldwide. Something of a natural klutz, he eventually breaks his various toys, though he has yet to break 100.

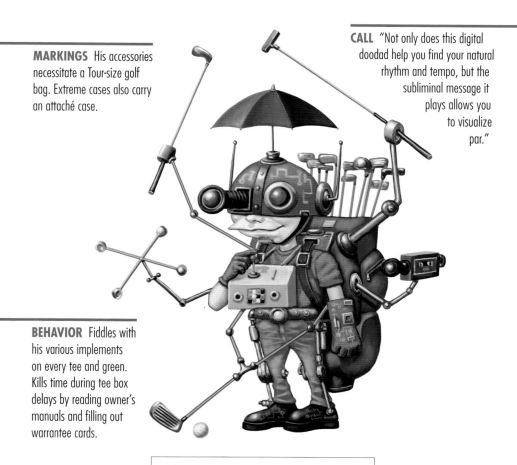

MARKINGS His accessories necessitate a Tour-size golf bag. Extreme cases also carry an attaché case.

CALL "Not only does this digital doodad help you find your natural rhythm and tempo, but the subliminal message it plays allows you to visualize par."

BEHAVIOR Fiddles with his various implements on every tee and green. Kills time during tee box delays by reading owner's manuals and filling out warrantee cards.

TECHNUS OBSESSUS

THE GAMBLER

Canis rogers 👉 There are few games more conducive to a friendly wager than golf. The handicap system is designed (sometimes abused—see the Sandbagger on page 66) so players of widely differing skill levels can enjoy a competitive match. Likewise, the endless permutations of golf competitions—Nassaus, Skins, Wolf, High-Low, 5-3-1, Bingo-Bango-Bongo—are just a quick half dozen of the ways players can make or lose a few bucks on the course. But the Gambler takes it to a different level. Most players love the game first and the action second. Not so this guy. He's all about the procurement of the greenback, be it on the greensward or the green felt of the gaming tables. His modus operandi is to parlay his greens fees into more green, and if the stakes are right (and he's an expert in making sure they are) he'll take on all comers, from the greenest Greenhorn (page 46) to the savviest of greenskeepers. Gamblers can be pleasant enough company, provided you watch your wallet as you watch this smoothie operate.

BEHAVIOR Intersperses flubbed sand shots and the occasional snap hook with a series of heat-seeking missiles at the flagstick.

MARKINGS Canvas bag, no-name equipment, leathery tan, carries a one-iron.

CALL "Maybe we should play for a little something. Just to keep it interesting."

CANIS ROGERS

MR. "GIMME"

Chronicus yips ☞ The sight of that small round hole, 4¼ inches in diameter, sends him into a panic. It doesn't much matter if he arrived on the green with a couple of high-quality swipes and is looking at a legitimate birdie chance. Or, as is usually the case, he "stick-handled" the ball up the fairway in wheezes, fits, and starts, and is trying to knock in a ten-footer for double bogey. The act of completion, of sending that Pinnacle plunging below ground, of hearing that sweet-sounding rattle at the bottom of the cup, makes him break into a cold sweat. He's gone from a standard-length putter to a belly putter planted in the abdomen to a long putter that rests beneath the chin. He's given up on conventional grips and latched onto Band-Aids like "the claw," or left-hand low, reverse overlap, profuse underbite, and any other gimmick of the month that might keep his total putts below fifty. And that's as apt a description as any for this sorry sack. A total putz.

MARKINGS Putts with glove on; uses oversize ball mark like a silver dollar or casino chip.

BEHAVIOR Rakes back anything under five feet, gives putts generously, both his own and opponents'.

CALL "Good, good?"

CHRONICUS YIPS

THE GOLF HOTTIE

Smoka allura ☞ She's as rare a sight as a double eagle, and just as welcoming. One of the reasons we love the game is because the courses are beautiful. But golf, unlike tennis, rarely attracts an abundance of beautiful women. Think about it: It's often a collection of struggling retirees, grim matrons, pinched professionals, hefty housewives, harried execs, earnest collegians, and wide-eyed teenagers. But how often do you see a set of gorgeous gams teetering on soft spikes? Wouldn't it be something if that ingenue striking range balls was striking in her own right? When was the last time you saw a gal swinging a golf club who looked like she spent her evenings swinging around a fire pole at a gentlemen's club? Try never. Ability is irrelevant. So is pace of play—take your time, sweetheart! And if her aptitude is nonexistent, etiquette lacking, and honesty in question, we don't really care. She may have a four-piece takeaway, but imagine her in a two-piece string bikini. And as long as she's using proper form as she bends to tee it up or fix her ball mark, then all is right in the golf world.

BEHAVIOR Sashays around the green; uses the ball washer provocatively.

MARKINGS Ideally, you can see the golf tees outlined in the back pocket of her shorts.

CALL "I'll hold your putter while you approach the hole."

SMOKA ALLURA

THE GREENHORN

Classis clueless ☛ Your golf career has to begin somewhere. When we learn the game, the first couple of fish-out-of-water rounds are an inevitability, a rite of passage. But why can some folks bluff more convincingly than others? Is it because they spent time on the range or taking lessons to prepare for their debut? Were they counseled by a wise golf daddy or older sibling? Did they get their feet wet (often literally) at the local pitch-and-putt beforehand? Do they just fake it well, knowing that even though it takes awhile to walk the walk, in the meantime they can talk the talk? The Greenhorn has trouble with the flagstick. He might pull it out and yank the cup cylinder out, too. He forgets to put the flag back in place, or leaves it listing at a 45 degree angle. He tees off from the wrong marker, takes practice swings dangerously close to his companions, and steps on balls in the rough. He casts shadows while you putt, tracks sand on the green after flailing from the bunker, and commits one faux pas after the next. The Greenhorn suffers golf growing pains. Too bad he can't grow more and be less of a pain.

MARKINGS Sneakers, sweatbands, mismatched irons.

BEHAVIOR Uses button on golf glove as ball mark, attempts to putt out of every bunker, uses stolen stripers for shots over water.

CALL "When I swing and miss, I don't count the stroke, 'cause I didn't hit it, right?"

CLASSIS CLUELESS

THE GURU

Solus intelligentus ☞ He's the picture-book example of the old adage "Those who can't do, teach." Few love the game more than the Guru, it's just he doesn't have an abundance of athletic ability or hand-eye coordination. Generally speaking, he couldn't hit snow if he slipped off an igloo. But just because he can't play a lick doesn't mean he can't help you, whether you want him to or not. With subscriptions to all the golf publications, videotapes of every Golf Channel instructional program of the last five years, and half a home library devoted to how-to golf tomes, no one knows more about the swing but is less qualified to impart this wisdom than your friendly Guru. Want to keep your golf game together? When you see this well-meaning nincompoop approaching, turn tail and run!

BEHAVIOR Breaks 90 twice a season, but can fix anyone else's flaws with a single perceptive comment.

MARKINGS Embroidered golf bag. Carries at least three wedges and two training devices.

CALL "You sure look out of alignment. Try strengthening your left-hand grip."

FIVE LESSONS
MY WAY
putting magic
DRIVING 101
LITTLE RED BOOK
SWING PHYSICS

SOLUS INTELLIGENTUS

THE INTROSPECT

Internus adspectus ☞ The classic moment in golf introspection history: It's 1947 and Claude Harmon is paired with Ben Hogan at the Masters. They're on arguably the most famous hole on the course, and one of the most renowned short par-3 holes in the world, Augusta National's dangerous 12th, called Golden Bell. Harmon makes an ace, the crowd goes wild, and Hogan never says a word. Walking off the green a few minutes later, Hogan turns to his playing companion and says, "You know, Claude, I've never made a two on that hole before." The Introspect isn't the worst guy to play golf with, at least not in comparison to the many other nefarious characters you can find. But if you choose to pay close attention to the self-flagellation or smug self-congratulations, the egocentric nature of his personality can wear you out quicker than a pair of two-dollar soft spikes on a concrete cart path. At least Hogan was a golf immortal, and one of the finest ball strikers in history. The Introspect you're stuck with probably has a "newspaper 9" handicap, and will legitimately break 80 about as often as the clocks change.

MARKINGS Chronic cases employ handheld tape recorders to document the highlights and oddities of the round to bore disinterested family members with later on.

CALL "But enough about me, let's talk about you. What do you think of my draw off of the tee? Have you noticed my improved short game?"

BEHAVIOR Brags about any shot he's executed with even a modicum of proficiency, explains his thought process and shares course-management technique to all within earshot.

INTERNUS ADSPECTUS

THE MULLIGAN MAN

Clintonicus ante foozle ☛ These were the kids who grew up screaming "Do-Over!" while playing kickball, freeze tag, or Simon Says, if the game wasn't proceeding to their liking. Later in life they tended to change college majors on a whim and either annul or opt for a quickie divorce if the marriage wasn't working. On the golf course they indulge in their own private version of "Instant Replay," and will rapid-fire a couple of shots in succession until they're satisfied with the end result. Or until they run out of balls, whichever comes first. Mulligan Men take their proverbs to heart, and their all-time favorite goes like this: "If at first you don't succeed, try, try, try, try, and try again."

BEHAVIOR Drops balls indiscriminately; appears to be sowing seeds like a latter-day Johnny Appleseed.

MARKINGS Extra tees behind the ears and in the shoelaces. An extra ball or two always at the ready.

CALL "That's how you're supposed to hit a seven-iron, for crying out loud. Why didn't I do that the first time?"

CLINTONICUS ANTE FOOZLE

THE NATURAL

Natura gifta ☞ We hackers, whackers, and slackers can't help but envy this rarest of species. Often they were high school stars and went on to become college players. Most were country club kids, their graceful motion honed under the watchful tutelage of the kindly old pro. He helped them develop their textbook posture with occasional lessons when they weren't busy on the tennis court, charging Dad's account at the snack bar, or lazing by the pool. Some still dabble in serious amateur competitions when away from their old-line country club. But most use their otherworldly talents to their advantage in the business world. You make quite the impression when you're breaking par, and they have the promotions, corner offices, and salaries to prove it. Bastards.

BEHAVIOR Silky-smooth move through the ball generates effortless power. Approaches float high and then drop gently near the pin. Safecracker's touch near the green.

MARKINGS Perfect swing, teeth. Unblemished skin, scorecard.

CALL "Caught that one on the screws, all right. Can't believe that eagle chip last hole hit the stick and stayed out."

NATURA GIFTA

THE NON-PLAYING WIFE

Spectator inertia 👉 Just so there are no charges of misogyny leveled, one can only assume that in the vast golf universe, somewhere there's a husband planted in the passenger seat of a golf buggy, watching passively as his wife chops and skitters her way across the greensward. But this vagabond golfer has never seen such a spectacle. What might possess a woman to waste four hours easing around in an E-Z-Go while hubby struggles to shoot a score a hairbreadth below triple digits? No clue. It's not as if a Non-Playing Wife has ever directly interfered with my game. But just like knowing there are Pauly Shore movies available for rent at the corner Blockbuster, it's the whole idea that bothers me. Not once have I observed a chronic cart dweller in possession of a book, magazine, or knitting needles. They just sit, stare at the scenery, and commiserate after the inevitable bad shot. Other than that, like the occasional one-iron you see popping up in someone's golf bag, they seem to serve no useful purpose.

MARKINGS Ample posterior, glazed countenance, often shod in a windbreaker.

BEHAVIOR Little to speak of. They stifle yawns, sip diet soft drinks, occasionally pencil in a 7 on the scorecard.

CALL "Honey, should I pull the cart around to the back of the green?"

SPECTATOR INERTIA

THE NOSTALGIC

Morpheus marcel proust ☞ "The older I get, the better I used to be" is the slogan for these mostly lovable louts. Not that the prerequisite for membership in this cult is necessarily an AARP card. You could be a college kid, playing during intersession for the first time since high school graduation. If you're signing for an 88, and lamenting the fact that you were rarely out of the 70s the spring you were named king of the prom, that makes you a bona fide Nostalgic. Compared to some of the fatuous fiends seen elsewhere in this guide, this fellow is harmless as a house cat. But if hole after mediocre hole is accompanied by a running commentary along the lines of, "You should've seen me yesterday," eventually he'll start to grate like fingernails on a chalkboard.

BEHAVIOR Struggling for bogeys while bragging about yesterday's birdies.

MARKINGS Faraway look in the eyes; commemorative Plexiglas scorecard attached to bag.

CALL "Would you believe I just skulled that into the other bunker? I had the same shot last week and blasted it out to a foot."

MORPHEUS MARCEL PROUST

MR. "PIDDLE-DOWN-THE-MIDDLE"

Terribilis vis ☞ No matter how erratic one's golf game may be, most reasonably competent players (someone who can break 100 at least some of the time) have the potential to reach almost all eighteen greens in regulation. Not so the Piddler. It might be age, infirmity, inflexibility, lack of physical strength, lousy technique, a skipped breakfast, or a crummy combination. But the fact remains that only about half of the holes on the course are reachable in regulation; the par-3s and shorter par-5s. Many of the par-4s are just too far down the fairway to be reached in two blows, because this anemic fellow lacks the length and strength to get it there. But you know what? He's straighter than Donny Osmond. He knocks it out of play every leap year, makes a mental error about as often as the Ryder Cup is played, and can get it up and down out of a washtub. You can hit a seven-wood farther than he hits a driver. But his handicap index is in the mid–single digits because he has far more birdies than blow-up holes and finishes below 80 twice as often as he's above 90. His game appears feeble. He looks frail. His metronomic consistency is frustrating. And in his own head-shaking way, he's fantastic.

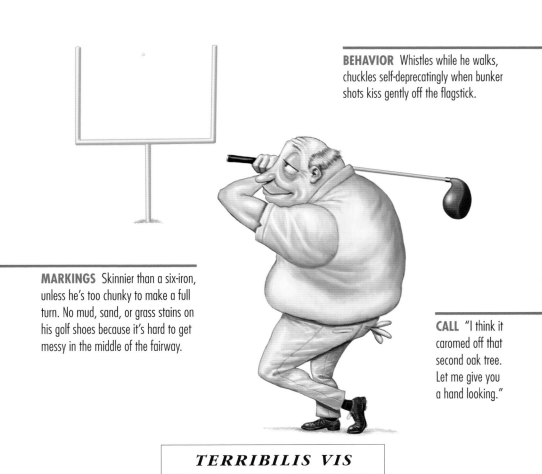

BEHAVIOR Whistles while he walks, chuckles self-deprecatingly when bunker shots kiss gently off the flagstick.

MARKINGS Skinnier than a six-iron, unless he's too chunky to make a full turn. No mud, sand, or grass stains on his golf shoes because it's hard to get messy in the middle of the fairway.

CALL "I think it caromed off that second oak tree. Let me give you a hand looking."

TERRIBILIS VIS

THE PRODIGY

Adulescens nonlaborus ☞ His youthful insouciance is maddening. Sure, he loves to play golf, but no more than video games, skateboarding, paintball, or hoops. In wintertime he zooms down the mountain on either skis or a snowboard; it doesn't matter. He doesn't have the money or the need for lessons, because whatever "it" is, he's got it. Even with a baseball grip and an extrawide stance, he belts it 290 yards off the tee. The Prodigy plays with the fearless abandon of youth. No fairway is too narrow, no water hazard too wide. He'll make a total shoulder turn, the swing as full and pretty as a rainbow, and loft a sky-high pitch shot from deep grass directly over the bunker that splats like bird droppings next to the flagstick. No need to baby that downhill nine-footer, he raps it smartly into the back of the cup. He gets around the course effortlessly, casually, playing as if he really doesn't care. You know what the secret is? He really doesn't.

BEHAVIOR Sends text messages while others are putting, plays Hacky Sack during tee box backups.

MARKINGS Surf-wear meets golf attire; Hawaiian print golf shirt usually untucked, grimy ball cap, no glove, no socks.

CALL "I don't really have any swing thoughts or mechanical keys. I just look at where I want the ball to go, step up, and hit it there."

ADULESCENS NONLABORUS

THE RULESMEISTER

Nerdus nebulous ☞ Much as he might've loved the sandlot football games in the neighborhood, Wiffle-ball contests in the neighbor's backyard, and kickball on the playground, he dreaded the choosing of sides. He was always picked dead last. It's a cruel irony that those who have the most desire so often have the least ability. His body couldn't respond to the challenges that sports required, but his nimble mind could. He played referee when unable to break into the sandlot lineup. As a teen he earned spending money as a Little League umpire and working the sidelines at youth soccer games. In short, he became a rules expert, and when his attention turned to golf as a young adult, he finally found a home. Unable to break 60 for nine holes without divine intervention, he immersed himself in the rule book. Just to stay in the game.

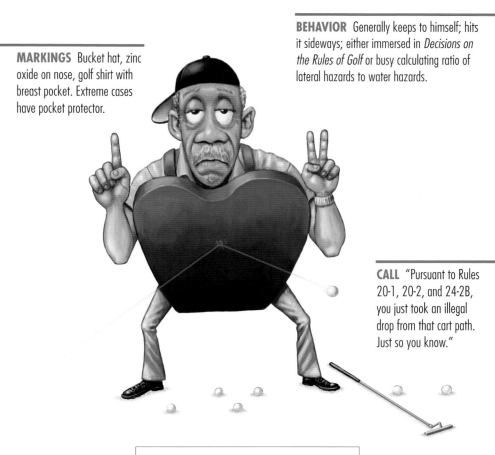

MARKINGS Bucket hat, zinc oxide on nose, golf shirt with breast pocket. Extreme cases have pocket protector.

BEHAVIOR Generally keeps to himself; hits it sideways; either immersed in *Decisions on the Rules of Golf* or busy calculating ratio of lateral hazards to water hazards.

CALL "Pursuant to Rules 20-1, 20-2, and 24-2B, you just took an illegal drop from that cart path. Just so you know."

NERDUS NEBULOUS

THE SANDBAGGER

Swindlus ceaseless ☞ It's a game chock-full of less-than-desirable practitioners, but truly, is there anyone, anything, worse than a classic Sandbagger? How low can you go, artificially inflating your handicap to win a logo visor, a pro-style umbrella, or a handful of measly pro shop chits? Then there's the equally abhorrent antipode, the vanity handicap. This charmer only posts his best scores, never entering the 95s and 98s because, "That's not how I usually play." So a chopper that's a legitimate 16 poses as an 11, gets killed in all the club tournaments, and drags his innocent and rule-abiding partner down with him. Both versions of this vermin should be keel-hauled through the scummiest water hazard on the course.

MARKINGS Wild version has squinty eyes and a two-iron; domestic version often characterized by mammoth Tour bag full of the latest high-tech rescue woods.

BEHAVIOR Claims he's not sure how a Nassau works; seems confused by the concept of presses.

CALL "Well, it sure was my lucky day. I've never reached a par-5 in two before!"

SWINDLUS CEASELESS

THE SLUGGARD

Latent lethargic ☛ When detractors make unflattering remarks about golf's inherent non-athleticism, this is the guy they're thinking of. It's not like he's been a couch potato his whole life, though. Many were fine athletes—perhaps high school quarterbacks or intramural basketball stars. But twenty-five years of televised sports, Tostitos, tater tots, T-bone steaks, triple scotches, and tequila shooters have taken half his energy, though he's literally twice the man he once was. But the competitor within still lurks below the expansive waistline. Golf is his game, though the idea of walking the course is as foreign a concept as a Caesar salad and mineral water at a business lunch.

BEHAVIOR Parks cart just out of backswing range to minimize walking distance; cruises rough in cart looking for lost balls, no matter how bumpy; pretends not to see CART PATH ONLY signs.

MARKINGS Massive golf bag, massive gut, shiny golf shoes.

CALL "If God had meant us to walk the golf course he wouldn't have invented poured concrete. Grab your wedge and putter. I'll bring it up to the green."

CART PATH ONLY

LATENT LETHARGIC

THE SNACKMAN

Doritos vulgaris 👉 A Snackman's prayer: Give us this golf day our daily bread. And lunch meat. And peanut butter crackers, a liter of Gatorade, and a king-sized Snickers. And hopefully more than just hot dogs at the turn—maybe a burrito station or pizza. There are folks who eat to live, others that live to eat, and hearty fellows like our Snackman, who live to eat on the links. What inspires this eighteen-course meal? It might be low blood sugar or low self-esteem. There's nothing inherently annoying about this mostly corpulent band of munchers, although it's a bummer when your partner blames his rotten approach shot on a slippery grip caused by dripping mayonnaise. But nobody wants to hear an apple crunching in their backswing or deal with a trail of dough-nut crumbs that impede a putting line. But they're a harmless bunch in comparison to some of the other reprehensible characters in this text. One word of caution does apply: Don't let a Snackman pick the golf venue. While most players select a course because of its historic significance, the architect's reputation, scenic vistas, ranking in the major golf magazines, or PGA Tour pedigree, these fellows have different priorities. They'll lead you to the links that feature a fresh sushi bar or slow-roast barbecue. Caveat emptor.

MARKINGS Crumbs on the chin; a paper napkin covers the golf shirt logo.

BEHAVIOR Spends an inordinate amount of time unwrapping, rearranging, dispensing, and disposing of his myriad comestibles.

CALL "Would you mind bringing my sandwich and butter? I mean, my sand wedge and putter?"

DORITOS VULGARIS

THE SPACE CADET

Gravitas zilch ☞ This unfortunate fellow leaves his mark in all walks of life, on and off the golf course. You'll see him aimlessly circling the mall parking lot, looking for his vehicle, in extreme moments of desperation asking passersby if they've seen a white Honda hatchback. He's been known to miss airline connections even though he arrived at gate twenty-seven in plenty of time. He was in terminal B instead of terminal D. He'll go to the baseball field to pick up Junior after practice, though his wife told him pointedly to fetch Missy at her music lesson. On the course it's more of the same. Though he's the only guy in the county still playing with fluorescent Top-Flites, he'll hit the wrong ball at least twice a round. Don't ask him to keep the scorecard; he'll screw it up. Don't ask him to drive the cart; he'll end up at the wrong hole. Don't ask him anything, except, "Isn't there medication available for people in your condition?"

BEHAVIOR Walks to the wrong cart; scatters his clubs; leaves the green clutching the flagstick.

MARKINGS Unzipped fly, mismatched socks, ball cap too big for his head.

CALL "What the heck? Anybody seen a five-iron?"

GRAVITAS ZILCH

THE STATUE

Rigorous mortis ☞ Why does an average round at an average course take five hours on average? The primary culprit is this miscreant. What she doesn't realize is that she could tally the exact same 118 in four hours, even three-and-a-half, as opposed to five. But watching Tour pros stalking putts from all angles, observing them in animated consultation with their caddies, seeing how they pay close and careful attention to the wind, the grain, and the scoreboard, have had a deleterious effect. What she hasn't managed to process is the fact that the men and women she sees on TV every weekend can calibrate shots to within three or four yards on almost every occasion, and each swing of the club can produce a paycheck variance worth many thousands of dollars. She, on the other hand, is lucky to get the ball airborne off the tee, rarely hits any shot farther than ninety yards, and plays for a nickel a hole. While the skills and the stakes aren't in the same galaxy as her heroes, one thing is: the miserable pace of play.

BEHAVIOR Like a bovine animal, appears to sleep standing up.

MARKINGS Grass in her shadow is often dormant from prolonged shade.

CALL "I'm not slow, it's just my pre-shot routine!"

RIGOROUS MORTIS

THE STORYTELLER

Prairie homo horribilis ☞ This misguided fellow is not to be confused with some of his close relations, namely the Chatterbox (page 20) and the Nostalgic (page 58). While the former spouts an unending series of rapid-fire non sequiturs and the latter confines his dialogue to tales of former glory, Story Boy walks a different path. He'll hold court on any and every subject that comes up in the round. If you mentioned you played Pebble Beach, he'll regale you with the time he *almost* got on Cypress Point. Made a killing on a Nasdaq sleeper? Wait till you hear how he cornered the pork belly market. Know a joke or two? Prepare for a game of "Can You Top This," because this gasbag knows a dozen good ones himself. The subject is irrelevant. You'll be subjected to his expertise on women ("I once dated a model that was so hot . . ."), spirits ("We had a $400 bottle of pinot noir the other night that was so good we ordered another . . ."), and travel ("Golf in Ireland is too much of a hassle unless you're using a helicopter . . ."). You'll be standing on the tee, listening to yet another fascinating tale with a silly grin plastered on your face, gripping your driver, thinking, "I'm just a couple over par, the foursome ahead is out of range, and I'm dying to bust this tee shot. Will this guy please shut up? Will he *ever* shut up?"

MARKINGS Golf shirt logo represents a well-known but exclusive private club. The "brag tags" culled from far-flung destinations dangling from his golf bag are as shiny and numerous as ornaments on a Christmas tree.

BEHAVIOR Quivers in anticipation as you come to the punch line of your favorite joke, so eager is he to tell a half dozen of his own.

CALL "So there I was, deep in the heart of the Congo . . ."

PRAIRIE HOMO HORRIBILIS

THE THINKER

Shoticus conundrum ☞ Even if you don't know the business end of a golf stick, you know this guy. He's the one that peppers the waitress with questions about the dinner special, wanting to know if the catch of the day is wild or farm raised, or if the green beans are sautéed in butter or olive oil. He kept the entire class in their seats during college, challenging the English professor's thesis, though the bell had already rung. He's the only guy who'll take the time to do a cost comparison of copying charges at both Kinko's and Mail Boxes Etc., factoring in the driving time and gas mileage to each location. On the golf course it's more of the same. He'll take a half dozen practice swings with the lob wedge, gauging the thickness of the rough. Then he'll sigh and repeat the process with the gap wedge. He'll walk the perimeter of the putting surface, vainly attempting to determine the "high" side of the green. In short, he's a pain in the ass.

MARKINGS Often carrying range finder, yardage guide, and wind gauge.

BEHAVIOR Paces off yardages compulsively, tears and tosses grass skyward even on chip shots.

CALL "Is it a hard five-iron or a soft four? Is that a crosswind or is it quartering?"

SHOTICUS CONUNDRUM

THE TIN WOODMAN

Homer formby ☞ This is a relatively new specimen, having only emerged on the golf course in the modern age of hybrid, or rescue, clubs. Just a few years ago, the vast majority of players carried a driver, three-wood, and maybe a five-wood. Then novelty clubs started to appear in weaker player's bags—the seven-wood, nine-wood, a short-shafted rescue club to escape punishing rough. Before too long these inveterate hackers were adding even more unwieldy masses of metal to their arsenal, replacing the elegant blades that had faithfully served generations of golfers before them. The sorriest of the lot have golf bags featuring more head covers than a synagogue during the high holidays. How much further can this pathetic envelope be pushed? A classic sand wedge should look like a scythe, but someday soon an avant-garde golf inventor will patent one that looks more like a Pepsi can on a stick.

MARKINGS The only blades in the bag belong to the putter and sand wedge. Perpetually rumpled and/or wrinkled, skin and otherwise.

BEHAVIOR Hits the driver off of the deck consistently and with impunity, chooses an eleven-wood on short par-3s, or a thirteen-wood if it's playing downwind.

CALL "I don't use an iron on my clothes. Why should I use one on the golf course?"

HOMER FORMBY

MY MISFITS MANIFESTO

MISFIT	NAME	OBSERVED AT
The Ball Hawk		
The Beverage Cart Kewpie		
Bigfoot		
The Boozehound		
The Caffeine Fiend		
The Career Caddie		
The Cart Gunner		
The Caveman		
The "Cell" Mate		
The Chatterbox		
The Cockeyed Optimist		
The Club Chucker		
The Collector		
The Cretin		
The Crybaby		
The Fair-Weather Fairy		
The Fashion Plate		
The Foot Wedger		
The Gadget Geek		
The Gambler		

MISFIT	NAME	OBSERVED AT
Mr. "Gimme"		
The Golf Hottie		
The Greenhorn		
The Guru		
The Introspect		
The Mulligan Man		
The Natural		
The Non-Playing Wife		
The Nostalgic		
Mr. "Piddle-Down-the-Middle"		
The Prodigy		
The Rulesmeister		
The Sandbagger		
The Sluggard		
The Snackman		
The Space Cadet		
The Statue		
The Storyteller		
The Thinker		
The Tin Woodman